PRINCEWILL LAGANG

Sands of Fortune: Secrets Behind Qatar's Wealth

First published by PRINCEWILL LAGANG 2023

Copyright © 2023 by Princewill Lagang

All rights reserved. No part of this publication may be reproduced, stored or transmitted in any form or by any means, electronic, mechanical, photocopying, recording, scanning, or otherwise without written permission from the publisher. It is illegal to copy this book, post it to a website, or distribute it by any other means without permission.

Princewill Lagang asserts the moral right to be identified as the author of this work.

First edition

This book was professionally typeset on Reedsy.
Find out more at reedsy.com

Contents

1. Sands of Fortune - Secrets Behind Qatar's Wealth — 1
2. From Deserts to Diversification - The Economic Miracle of... — 4
3. Bridging the Past and the Future - Qatar's Cultural... — 7
4. Qatar's Global Ambitions - Diplomacy, Sports, and Soft Power — 10
5. Challenges and Aspirations - Navigating the Future — 13
6. Qatar's Global Footprint - A Shaping Force on the World... — 16
7. Qatar and the Future - Navigating the Unknown — 19
8. Qatar's Enduring Legacy - Reflections and Future Horizons — 22
9. A World Transformed - Qatar's Global Impact — 24
10. A Vision for the Future - Qatar's Endless Journey — 27
11. The World Transformed - Qatar's Legacy in the Global Context — 29
12. A Continuing Odyssey - Qatar's Journey Never Ends — 31
13. Summary — 33

1

Sands of Fortune - Secrets Behind Qatar's Wealth

The sun hung low in the Arabian sky, casting long shadows over the sprawling city of Doha. Towering glass skyscrapers glinted like shards of crystal in the scorching desert heat, a testament to the opulence and ambition of this tiny Gulf nation. The hustle and bustle of the streets below was a stark contrast to the vast, golden sands that stretched into infinity, providing the backdrop for the awe-inspiring wealth that had transformed Qatar into a global financial powerhouse.

In a country that had only recently emerged from obscurity, its meteoric rise to prosperity had become a subject of worldwide fascination. The glittering skyline of Doha, the luxurious shopping malls, and the extravagant lifestyles of its citizens all hinted at the vast reservoir of wealth hidden beneath the surface. But what were the secrets behind Qatar's unparalleled riches, and how had this nation, no larger than the state of Connecticut, managed to accumulate such staggering wealth in such a short span of time?

To understand Qatar's ascent to prosperity, one must look back to the nation's humble origins. A mere half-century ago, Qatar was a desolate and largely impoverished desert emirate with a population that relied on fishing, pearl diving, and a modicum of agriculture for survival. The discovery of vast oil and natural gas reserves beneath the Arabian sands would forever alter the course of this nation's history.

In the early 20th century, while the world was embroiled in two devastating world wars, Qatar's strategic importance as a British protectorate was solidified due to its maritime location and oil potential. It wasn't until the 1940s and 1950s, however, that the real transformation began. Qatar's oil reserves were proven to be substantial, and foreign companies flocked to the tiny peninsula. In 1950, the Qatar Petroleum Company was formed, marking the first significant step toward economic growth.

Within a few decades, Qatar had transitioned from a struggling backwater into a global energy giant. The country's vast reserves of oil and natural gas had been harnessed to power the nation's rapid development. Foreign expertise and investment had played a pivotal role in unlocking this wealth, with multinational corporations sharing the profits and technological advancements necessary for the extraction and exportation of these valuable resources.

It was during this period that the Al Thani family, the ruling dynasty of Qatar, consolidated their power and managed the nation's newfound riches with a deft hand. Sheikh Hamad bin Khalifa Al Thani's 1995 coup d'état, which saw him seize power from his father, marked the beginning of an era of profound transformation and modernization. He embraced a vision of Qatar as a global player on the world stage, and his son, Sheikh Tamim bin Hamad Al Thani, continued that legacy.

But Qatar's ascent to global prominence wasn't solely about oil and gas. The nation's leadership recognized the finite nature of these resources and embarked on a diversification strategy. The Qatar Investment Authority

(QIA), established in 2005, became the primary vehicle for managing the nation's wealth and investments. The QIA's portfolio included investments in global companies, real estate ventures, and a growing media empire. The acquisition of prestigious assets such as Harrods in London and significant stakes in companies like Volkswagen and Barclays showcased Qatar's ambition and financial clout.

Qatar also made significant investments in education and culture. The creation of Education City, home to various international universities and research centers, symbolized the nation's commitment to nurturing knowledge and innovation. Hosting global sporting events like the 2006 Asian Games and the upcoming 2022 FIFA World Cup added to Qatar's reputation as a world-class destination.

As the chapter unfolds, we will delve deeper into the secrets behind Qatar's wealth, from its successful diplomacy and strategic investments to its visionary leadership and ambitious vision for the future. We will explore the nation's cultural renaissance and its embrace of technology and innovation, all of which have contributed to Qatar's incredible journey from a barren desert to a global economic powerhouse. Through these revelations, we aim to unravel the enigmatic "Sands of Fortune" and shed light on the extraordinary transformation of Qatar.

2

From Deserts to Diversification - The Economic Miracle of Qatar

The sun dipped below the horizon, painting the desert landscape in hues of deep orange and fiery red. As the day gave way to night, the city of Doha came alive with a different kind of energy. For Qatar, the night was when the true wealth of the nation was most evident, where the gleaming lights of its skyscrapers symbolized not only its prosperity but also its remarkable transformation over the decades.

Qatar's wealth was no longer solely dependent on the whims of the oil market. The leadership had learned from the volatile lessons of the past, and they were determined to safeguard the nation's future. This chapter delves into the economic diversification strategy that had become the cornerstone of Qatar's success.

The 1970s marked a period of significant growth for Qatar. The rapid development of its oil and gas sector brought a flood of revenue, but the leadership knew they needed to do more than rely on finite fossil fuels. Qatar's oil and gas reserves, while substantial, would eventually run dry. As a result, they set out on a mission to diversify the economy and invest in non-energy sectors.

One of the most notable milestones in this journey was the establishment of the Qatar Financial Centre (QFC) in 2005. The QFC sought to attract international financial institutions, insurance companies, and other service providers by offering an attractive regulatory environment. It created a thriving financial hub within the nation, contributing to Qatar's stature as a regional economic powerhouse.

Qatar's leadership also recognized the potential of its national airline, Qatar Airways, as a global brand. The airline's rapid expansion and the development of Hamad International Airport in Doha positioned Qatar as a vital player in the aviation industry. Qatar Airways became a key driver of both tourism and trade.

As the chapter unfolds, we will explore how the state-controlled sovereign wealth fund, the Qatar Investment Authority (QIA), played a pivotal role in Qatar's economic diversification strategy. The QIA's astute investments in international companies, luxury real estate, and iconic assets further solidified Qatar's presence on the global stage.

Additionally, we will examine the significance of Education City, a visionary project that brought leading international universities to Qatar. This initiative was instrumental in nurturing a knowledge-based economy, fostering innovation, and creating a skilled workforce capable of driving the nation's ambitious agenda.

Cultural investments were also part of Qatar's diversification strategy. World-class museums, such as the Museum of Islamic Art and the National Museum of Qatar, showcased the nation's rich history and commitment to cultural preservation. These institutions attracted global attention and contributed to Qatar's soft power on the world stage.

Qatar's pursuit of technology and innovation was not left behind either. Initiatives such as Qatar Science & Technology Park (QSTP) and its investments in emerging technologies were integral in shaping Qatar's role in the Fourth Industrial Revolution.

Throughout this chapter, we will uncover the multifaceted approach that transformed Qatar from a nation reliant on oil and gas into a diversified, economically resilient, and forward-looking nation. The story of Qatar's economic miracle is a testament to visionary leadership, strategic planning, and a relentless commitment to securing a prosperous future for generations to come.

3

Bridging the Past and the Future - Qatar's Cultural Renaissance

The gentle breeze off the Arabian Gulf carried the scent of saltwater as it whispered through the bustling streets of Souq Waqif, Doha's vibrant marketplace. Amidst the labyrinthine alleyways, merchants displayed their wares, a colorful tapestry of fabrics, spices, jewelry, and handicrafts. This was the heart of Qatar's cultural renaissance, where the past intertwined with the future, a testament to the nation's commitment to preserving its rich heritage.

Qatar's journey to cultural renaissance was not just about preserving history but also about breathing new life into it. The nation was determined to build a bridge between its ancient traditions and the modern world. The ambitious cultural projects that unfolded in the early 21st century were a reflection of this vision.

One of the most iconic symbols of Qatar's cultural revival was the Museum of Islamic Art (MIA), a stunning architectural masterpiece designed by I. M. Pei. This institution was more than just a museum; it was a statement of Qatar's commitment to celebrating Islamic heritage. Inside, an exquisite collection of Islamic art spanning centuries and continents was on display, showcasing the intricate craftsmanship and artistic achievements of the Islamic world.

The National Museum of Qatar, a work of architectural genius designed by Jean Nouvel, was another marvel. Its structure, inspired by the crystalline forms of desert roses, told the story of Qatar, from its ancient Bedouin roots to its modern transformation. The museum's immersive exhibits and multimedia displays offered a glimpse into the nation's history and culture, providing a vivid backdrop to the unfolding narrative of Qatar's identity.

Qatar's love for the arts was not confined to museums alone. The establishment of the Qatar Philharmonic Orchestra and the Qatar National Library added a new dimension to the cultural landscape. These institutions nurtured local talent while inviting international artists to share their expertise and knowledge. The Doha Film Institute contributed to Qatar's growing influence in the world of cinema by hosting the annual Ajyal Youth Film Festival and funding groundbreaking cinematic ventures.

Beyond the realm of the arts, Qatar made significant efforts to preserve its intangible cultural heritage. Initiatives to document and promote traditional Qatari crafts, such as Al Sadu weaving and pearl diving, helped keep age-old traditions alive in a rapidly changing world.

Cultural diplomacy also played a crucial role in Qatar's journey. Hosting the Doha Debates, the annual World Innovation Summit for Education (WISE), and the Doha Forum allowed the nation to become a global platform for dialogue and exchange of ideas. The Qatar Foundation, established in 1995, served as the cornerstone for these initiatives, fostering education and research while promoting cultural understanding.

This chapter will explore Qatar's cultural renaissance in depth, delving into the nation's commitment to both preserving its heritage and fostering new creative horizons. It will showcase how Qatar's cultural investments not only enriched the nation's cultural landscape but also strengthened its influence on the global stage, making Qatar a beacon of art, history, and innovation in the Gulf region and beyond. The story of Qatar's cultural renaissance is a story of embracing the past while reaching for a brighter future, and it continues to inspire people both within and beyond its borders.

4

Qatar's Global Ambitions - Diplomacy, Sports, and Soft Power

The beating heart of a nation is not confined to its geography; it extends to the relationships it forges with the world. For Qatar, a small but immensely influential Gulf state, the quest for global recognition and influence was a multifaceted journey. Chapter 4 unveils Qatar's diplomatic and soft power strategies, highlighting how they leveraged global events and investments in sports, media, and humanitarian initiatives to propel the nation onto the world stage.

In the late 20th century, Qatar's leadership realized that diplomacy was a powerful tool for enhancing the nation's global prominence. The Qatari government adeptly navigated regional and international politics, maintaining stable relationships with countries across the spectrum. Qatar's policy of non-interference and mediation in regional conflicts garnered respect, culminating in the brokering of peace deals and negotiations that resolved crises in the Middle East.

The 2022 FIFA World Cup bid was a turning point in Qatar's global ambitions. The world's most-watched sporting event presented an unparalleled opportunity to showcase the nation's capabilities. Qatar's successful bid and subsequent preparations for the tournament were a testament to their vision and resources. State-of-the-art stadiums, modern infrastructure, and ambitious hospitality projects made Qatar a sports destination like no other.

Hosting the World Cup was not just about sports; it was a grand spectacle designed to leave an indelible mark on the global imagination. Qatar utilized this event to showcase its cutting-edge technology, commitment to sustainability, and drive to create a legacy beyond the tournament. The stadiums were designed with energy efficiency in mind, and the tournament's branding celebrated Qatar's rich cultural heritage, ensuring a lasting impact.

Soft power was a crucial aspect of Qatar's global strategy. The nation invested heavily in the media, including the international news network Al Jazeera, which revolutionized the way news was reported in the Middle East and beyond. Qatar's media ventures not only provided a platform for the nation's perspective but also helped shape global narratives.

Humanitarian initiatives, like the Qatar Fund for Development, played a pivotal role in soft power projection. The nation's contributions to disaster relief, education, and healthcare around the world enhanced its image as a responsible and compassionate global actor.

Qatar's vision extended to higher education as well. Education City, home to prominent international universities, brought students and researchers from across the globe to Qatar, fostering cross-cultural exchanges and promoting a forward-thinking, knowledge-based society.

This chapter will explore how Qatar's global ambitions, shaped by astute diplomacy, strategic investments, and the hosting of high-profile events, propelled it onto the global stage. Qatar's commitment to being a responsible and influential actor on the world scene underscores the nation's belief in the power of diplomacy, sports, media, and humanitarian efforts to reshape the global order and secure its place in the world. The story of Qatar's global ambitions is a testament to its vision, leadership, and ability to seize opportunities on the world stage.

5

Challenges and Aspirations - Navigating the Future

The relentless heat of the Qatari desert cast long shadows over the glistening skyline of Doha as the nation approached the third decade of the 21st century. Qatar's journey had been one of remarkable transformation, yet it was not without its challenges and uncertainties. As the nation looked toward the future, this chapter explores the hurdles Qatar faced, its aspirations, and the strategies it envisioned for the road ahead.

One of the pressing challenges Qatar grappled with was the need to diversify its economy further. Despite its successes, the nation remained heavily reliant on oil and gas revenues. The leadership was well aware that these finite resources could not sustain Qatar's future indefinitely. The drive to foster a knowledge-based economy, spur innovation, and continue investing in non-energy sectors became paramount.

The blockade imposed on Qatar by its neighboring states in 2017 was a test of the nation's resilience. In the face of diplomatic isolation, Qatar demonstrated its ability to adapt and find alternative solutions. The crisis led to a renewed emphasis on self-sufficiency and the development of key sectors like agriculture, where Qatar aimed to reduce its reliance on food imports and enhance its food security.

Sustainability was also at the forefront of Qatar's agenda. The nation had made significant strides in addressing environmental challenges, including water scarcity and energy consumption. Investments in renewable energy, such as solar power, and the expansion of desalination plants marked a commitment to a greener future.

Qatar's population was growing rapidly, largely due to the influx of expatriate workers and their families. Ensuring the well-being and integration of these communities was essential. Reforms aimed at improving labor rights and living conditions for foreign workers were part of the broader vision of social progress.

Qatar's global engagement was another priority. The nation sought to expand its role as a mediator in regional conflicts, contribute to peacekeeping efforts, and work toward a more stable Middle East. Qatar's involvement in humanitarian initiatives and foreign aid continued to be a cornerstone of its diplomacy.

This chapter also explores Qatar's aspirations in sports, arts, and culture. Beyond hosting the 2022 FIFA World Cup, the nation aimed to become a sporting hub by hosting international tournaments, including the 2030 Asian Games. Qatar's thriving arts and culture scene was set to grow with the completion of various cultural projects, such as the Qatar National Museum and the National Library.

As the chapter unfolds, we delve into Qatar's vision for the future and the strategies it adopted to navigate the challenges of the 21st century. The nation's resilience, adaptability, and forward-thinking leadership make Qatar a compelling case study in confronting adversity and continuing its journey toward a prosperous and sustainable future. Qatar's story serves as an inspiration for nations worldwide that seek to surmount obstacles and embrace a path of growth, development, and progress.

6

Qatar's Global Footprint - A Shaping Force on the World Stage

In the early decades of the 21st century, Qatar had evolved from a small, relatively unknown Gulf nation into a formidable global player. The nation's influence had expanded far beyond its borders, and its vision, diplomacy, and wealth made it a significant shaping force on the world stage. This chapter delves into the various ways Qatar projected its influence globally, from political and economic alliances to humanitarian efforts and beyond.

One of the most striking manifestations of Qatar's global impact was its role in international diplomacy. Qatar had become a trusted mediator and peacemaker, involving itself in numerous regional conflicts. The 2019 U.S.-Taliban peace talks hosted in Doha were a testament to the nation's diplomatic prowess. These negotiations aimed to bring an end to the conflict in Afghanistan, highlighting Qatar's role in shaping the peace process in one of the most complex conflicts of the 21st century.

Qatar was also an active participant in the Gulf Cooperation Council (GCC), working with its neighbors to address regional challenges and build economic and political unity. However, it was not without its share of regional tensions, particularly in the aftermath of the 2017 blockade imposed by some GCC members. Qatar's approach to resolving these issues, primarily through dialogue and diplomacy, underscored its commitment to regional stability.

Economically, Qatar's global reach was extensive. The Qatar Investment Authority (QIA) continued to make strategic investments worldwide, shaping global markets and industries. The nation's stake in prominent companies, real estate, and infrastructure projects across the globe made Qatar a significant player in the international economic landscape.

Humanitarian efforts were an integral part of Qatar's global identity. The Qatar Fund for Development, alongside organizations like Qatar Charity, played a crucial role in providing aid and relief to countries in need. Whether responding to natural disasters or supporting development projects, Qatar's humanitarian initiatives made a profound impact in various parts of the world.

Qatar's aspiration to become a global hub for education and research had borne fruit. Education City, with its esteemed international universities and research institutions, attracted students and scholars from all corners of the world. This academic diversity not only contributed to Qatar's global standing but also fostered cross-cultural exchanges and knowledge sharing.

The nation's sporting ambitions were no less impressive. Hosting the 2022 FIFA World Cup was a monumental achievement, and Qatar aimed to build on its success by becoming a global sports destination. The bid for the 2030 Asian Games and continued investments in sports infrastructure highlighted Qatar's commitment to sports as a means of enhancing its global footprint.

In this chapter, we explore how Qatar's influence extended far beyond its borders, showcasing the nation's role as a shaping force on the world stage.

The story of Qatar's global footprint is one of diplomacy, economic acumen, humanitarian commitment, and cultural exchange, all of which have solidified Qatar's place in the international community as a nation that influences and inspires.

7

Qatar and the Future - Navigating the Unknown

As the 21st century marched forward, Qatar stood at the crossroads of immense opportunities and unprecedented challenges. In this chapter, we delve into the nation's strategies, aspirations, and resilience as it embarked on the next phase of its journey, navigating the complexities of an ever-changing global landscape.

The global energy landscape was undergoing a profound transformation, with a growing emphasis on sustainability and renewable energy sources. Qatar, a major player in the oil and gas industry, recognized the importance of diversifying its energy portfolio. Investments in renewable energy, such as solar power and the development of a hydrogen economy, showcased Qatar's commitment to sustainability and its intention to remain a key energy supplier in the evolving energy market.

Qatar continued to invest in diversifying its economy, with a particular focus on knowledge-based industries. Initiatives aimed at fostering innovation, entrepreneurship, and research and development were pivotal to this endeavor.

The country's thriving technology sector, research institutions, and startup ecosystem were vital components in securing its economic future.

In the realm of diplomacy, Qatar remained a key mediator in regional conflicts and a voice for peace. The nation sought to strengthen its alliances while playing an active role in addressing the geopolitical challenges of the region. Qatar's global diplomatic outreach extended to fostering relations with nations worldwide, contributing to peace and stability.

Building on the legacy of the 2022 FIFA World Cup, Qatar continued to position itself as a sports hub. Hosting the 2030 Asian Games and investing in sports infrastructure were steps toward solidifying its status as a global sports destination.

Cultural aspirations were not left behind either. Qatar's flourishing arts and culture scene saw the completion of various cultural projects, including the National Museum and the National Library. These institutions aimed to showcase Qatar's rich heritage and contribute to the nation's soft power on the world stage.

Education and research remained a priority, with Education City evolving to attract leading institutions from around the world. This academic hub was instrumental in fostering global collaborations and nurturing the next generation of leaders and thinkers.

The chapter also delves into the nation's response to regional challenges and conflicts, emphasizing Qatar's commitment to dialogue, diplomacy, and peaceful resolution. The story of Qatar's continued evolution is a testament to its visionary leadership, resilience, and determination to navigate the unknown.

As the final chapter in the story of Qatar's remarkable journey, we explore how the nation adapted to the changing tides of the 21st century and remained a beacon of progress, resilience, and hope in an ever-evolving world. Qatar's story is one of a nation that dared to dream, and, through astute leadership and strategic vision, transformed those dreams into reality.

8

Qatar's Enduring Legacy - Reflections and Future Horizons

As the story of Qatar's remarkable journey unfolds, the nation reached a pivotal moment in its history. This concluding chapter reflects on the enduring legacy of Qatar and looks toward the future horizons that lay ahead. It explores the lessons learned, the challenges overcome, and the aspirations that continue to drive the nation forward.

Qatar's legacy was one of extraordinary transformation. From a small, desert emirate to a global player on the world stage, the nation had overcome numerous obstacles. The story of Qatar was a testament to visionary leadership, strategic planning, and the unyielding determination to secure a prosperous and sustainable future.

The nation's diversification efforts had borne fruit, creating a knowledge-based economy, fostering innovation, and embracing sustainability. Qatar had learned to adapt to the shifting global energy landscape, becoming a player in renewable energy sources and emerging as a key contributor to the world's energy transition.

QATAR'S ENDURING LEGACY - REFLECTIONS AND FUTURE HORIZONS

In the realm of diplomacy, Qatar's role as a mediator and peacemaker had made a significant impact on regional and international conflicts. The nation had demonstrated the power of dialogue and diplomacy in resolving complex geopolitical challenges, contributing to peace and stability.

Culturally, Qatar had become a vibrant hub for arts, culture, and education. Iconic institutions like the Museum of Islamic Art, the National Museum of Qatar, and Education City celebrated the nation's rich heritage while fostering cross-cultural exchange and knowledge sharing.

Sports had become a central pillar of Qatar's identity, with the successful hosting of the 2022 FIFA World Cup and plans for the 2030 Asian Games solidifying the nation's position as a global sports destination.

The nation's humanitarian efforts, through organizations like the Qatar Fund for Development and Qatar Charity, had extended a helping hand to countries in need, making a positive impact around the world.

As Qatar looked to the future, the chapter explored the nation's aspirations for continued growth, progress, and global influence. The challenges that lay ahead were acknowledged, but Qatar's history had shown that it possessed the vision, resources, and resilience to overcome them.

The story of Qatar was one of inspiration, not just for the nation itself but for countries around the world seeking to transform their destinies. Qatar's journey served as a testament to the power of visionary leadership, strategic planning, and a relentless commitment to securing a prosperous and sustainable future for generations to come. The chapter concluded by highlighting the endless potential and future horizons that lay before Qatar, a nation with a legacy that would continue to inspire and shape the world.

9

A World Transformed - Qatar's Global Impact

The story of Qatar's remarkable journey would not be complete without an exploration of the global impact the nation had on the world. As Qatar continued to evolve, its influence extended beyond its borders, touching diverse aspects of the international stage. This chapter delves into the far-reaching consequences of Qatar's actions, policies, and initiatives on a global scale.

Qatar's role as a key mediator in regional and international conflicts had profound implications for global peace and security. The nation's diplomatic endeavors yielded significant results, from the successful brokering of peace agreements to the resolution of long-standing disputes. By embracing dialogue and diplomacy as a means of conflict resolution, Qatar set an example for nations worldwide.

The hosting of major international events, particularly the 2022 FIFA World Cup and the planned 2030 Asian Games, had a transformative effect on the global sports landscape. Qatar's investments in sports infrastructure and its commitment to fostering a culture of physical activity left an indelible mark on the world of sports, inspiring nations to enhance their own sports initiatives.

Qatar's investments in renewable energy sources, such as solar power and the hydrogen economy, marked a pivotal moment in the global energy transition. As the world grappled with the challenges of climate change and sustainability, Qatar's commitment to clean and renewable energy set a powerful example for other nations to follow, promoting a more sustainable and environmentally friendly future.

The nation's cultural achievements and initiatives, including world-class museums and education institutions, contributed to the enrichment of global culture and the promotion of cross-cultural understanding. Qatar's investments in the arts, education, and heritage preservation encouraged other nations to prioritize cultural development and preservation.

In the field of humanitarian efforts, Qatar's contributions to disaster relief, healthcare, and development projects significantly impacted the well-being of people around the world. The Qatar Fund for Development and Qatar Charity were not only symbols of Qatar's generosity but also inspired others to engage in philanthropy and humanitarian work.

The global reach of Qatar's media empire, particularly through Al Jazeera, transformed the landscape of international journalism and news dissemination. The network's role in providing alternative perspectives and facilitating global discourse had a lasting impact on the media industry.

This chapter serves as a testament to Qatar's influence on the world, both in terms of tangible achievements and the inspiration it provided to nations seeking to make a positive difference on the global stage. Qatar's story is not just one of a nation's transformation but a narrative of a nation that, through its vision and actions, had a profound impact on the world, reshaping the global landscape in numerous ways.

10

A Vision for the Future - Qatar's Endless Journey

In the final chapter of Qatar's remarkable journey, we look ahead to the nation's vision for the future, recognizing that Qatar's story is not static but ever-evolving. The future holds boundless possibilities, challenges, and aspirations, and Qatar's commitment to progress, sustainability, and global influence remains unwavering.

Qatar's ongoing commitment to diversifying its economy beyond fossil fuels defines its vision for the future. The nation's investments in knowledge-based industries, technology, and innovation will continue to drive economic growth, ensuring a prosperous and sustainable future for its citizens.

In the face of global challenges, particularly those related to climate change and environmental sustainability, Qatar's investments in renewable energy sources and environmental initiatives reflect its dedication to a greener and more sustainable future. The nation aims to be a pioneer in the global transition to clean energy and ecological responsibility.

As Qatar continues to host major international events, its ambition is to leave a lasting legacy beyond the tournaments themselves. The 2022 FIFA World Cup and the planned 2030 Asian Games are opportunities to showcase the nation's capacity for innovation, sustainability, and sportsmanship, setting new standards for future global sporting events.

Cultural development remains a cornerstone of Qatar's vision for the future. The nation's commitment to preserving its heritage, fostering the arts, and promoting education ensures that Qatar will continue to enrich global culture and cross-cultural understanding.

Humanitarian efforts and philanthropy will remain integral to Qatar's global engagement, with organizations like the Qatar Fund for Development and Qatar Charity continuing to make a positive impact on the lives of people around the world.

In the realm of diplomacy, Qatar's role as a mediator and peacemaker is set to expand as it tackles the challenges of regional conflicts and works toward global peace and security. Qatar's commitment to dialogue and diplomacy is unwavering, and its influence on the international stage is set to grow.

The future of education in Qatar holds great promise, with Education City evolving as a global hub for knowledge exchange, research, and cross-cultural collaboration. By nurturing the next generation of thinkers, Qatar is ensuring a bright future for itself and the world.

In this concluding chapter, we reflect on Qatar's unwavering commitment to progress, sustainability, and global influence. The nation's story is not one of a static past but an endless journey of vision, determination, and an unyielding belief in a prosperous and sustainable future. Qatar's story is a beacon of hope and inspiration for nations worldwide, a testament to the power of vision, leadership, and resilience in shaping a better future for all.

11

The World Transformed - Qatar's Legacy in the Global Context

As we delve into the final chapter of Qatar's extraordinary journey, it's time to reflect on the nation's legacy in the global context. Qatar's impact has transcended its borders and influenced the world in multifaceted ways. In this chapter, we consider the broader implications of Qatar's story and the lessons it offers to the global community.

Diplomatically, Qatar's role as a mediator and peacemaker in regional and international conflicts has demonstrated the power of dialogue and diplomacy in resolving complex geopolitical challenges. Its contributions to global peace and security continue to shape the world's approach to conflict resolution.

The hosting of major international events, notably the 2022 FIFA World Cup and the planned 2030 Asian Games, has left a profound mark on the global sports landscape. These events have redefined the standards for hosting major tournaments, emphasizing sustainability, innovation, and accessibility, and inspiring other nations to follow suit.

Qatar's commitment to renewable energy and environmental sustainability serves as a model for the world as countries grapple with the challenges of climate change. The nation's investments in clean energy sources and its transition to a hydrogen economy underscore the importance of adopting eco-friendly practices for a sustainable future.

Culturally, Qatar's contributions to the arts, education, and heritage preservation have enriched global culture and promoted cross-cultural understanding. By nurturing institutions like the Museum of Islamic Art, the National Museum of Qatar, and Education City, Qatar has set an example for celebrating cultural heritage and fostering a culture of learning and exchange.

Qatar's philanthropic initiatives and humanitarian efforts, facilitated through organizations like the Qatar Fund for Development and Qatar Charity, have had a transformative effect on people's lives worldwide. These efforts underscore the importance of global collaboration in addressing humanitarian challenges.

In the media industry, Qatar's global influence through Al Jazeera and other media outlets has redefined the landscape of international journalism. Qatar's role in facilitating global discourse and providing alternative perspectives has left an indelible impact on the media industry.

This chapter aims to highlight Qatar's global legacy and its contributions to the world, providing valuable lessons and insights for nations and individuals alike. Qatar's story is a testament to the potential of vision, leadership, and resilience in shaping a better future for all. It underscores the capacity of a small nation to leave an enduring impact on the global stage, serving as a source of inspiration for the world.

12

A Continuing Odyssey - Qatar's Journey Never Ends

As we reach the final chapter of Qatar's remarkable journey, it becomes clear that this is not the end but a transition to the next chapter of a story that will continue to evolve. Qatar's odyssey is a testament to its commitment to progress, innovation, and a brighter future for its citizens and the world. In this concluding chapter, we explore the concept that Qatar's journey never truly ends, and that the nation's vision for the future is a beacon that will guide it on this unending voyage.

The story of Qatar serves as a powerful reminder that a nation's journey is a perpetual one. While accomplishments are celebrated, lessons are learned from challenges and achievements alike. Qatar's path has shown that the pursuit of excellence and progress is not a destination but a continuous process.

The nation's commitment to diversifying its economy, investing in renewable energy, and embracing sustainability represents an ongoing mission. The journey toward economic diversification and environmental responsibility is an enduring one, marked by constant adaptation to a changing world.

The global impact of Qatar, whether through diplomatic mediation, hosting major international events, promoting renewable energy, or enriching global culture, is part of an ongoing narrative. The nation's influence on the world stage will only grow in significance as it continues to navigate complex global challenges.

In the future, Qatar's leadership and people will remain dedicated to the principles that have guided the nation thus far. The unwavering commitment to knowledge, innovation, and humanitarian efforts will continue to shape Qatar's narrative and influence the world.

Qatar's vision for the future, as outlined in this chapter, will ensure that the nation remains a beacon of hope and inspiration, not only for its own citizens but for the global community. The story of Qatar is a testament to the power of vision, leadership, and resilience, serving as an enduring source of inspiration for nations and individuals around the world.

As we conclude this epic journey, it becomes evident that the story of Qatar is not bound by the confines of a book. Instead, it is a living testament to the enduring spirit of progress and the indomitable human will to shape a better future. Qatar's odyssey is an inspiration to all who seek to create a brighter, more sustainable world for generations to come.

13

Summary

In this extensive narrative spanning twelve chapters, we've explored the incredible journey of Qatar, a small Gulf nation that evolved into a global player on the world stage. Qatar's story is a testament to visionary leadership, strategic planning, and an unyielding commitment to securing a prosperous and sustainable future.

The story begins with an introduction to Qatar, its historical roots, and the geographic and cultural elements that shaped the nation. We then delve into Qatar's transition from a modest desert emirate to an economic powerhouse, primarily driven by its oil and gas wealth.

As the narrative unfolds, we witness Qatar's commitment to diversify its economy, investing in non-energy sectors, creating a thriving financial hub, and establishing a global airline. Education City and cultural institutions celebrate Qatar's heritage while fostering innovation and knowledge-based industries.

The story delves into Qatar's diplomatic efforts, highlighting its role as a mediator in regional conflicts and a contributor to global peace. The hosting of the 2022 FIFA World Cup and the 2030 Asian Games underscores the nation's ambition to be a global sports destination.

The chapter on Qatar's global ambitions showcases its involvement in regional diplomacy, the development of its media industry, and its role as a humanitarian and educational hub. The subsequent chapters delve into the nation's enduring legacy, exploring the implications of its actions, from diplomacy to sports, cultural development, and humanitarian efforts.

In the final chapters, we glimpse Qatar's vision for the future, emphasizing sustainability, renewable energy, and its commitment to ongoing economic diversification. The narrative underscores Qatar's leadership in a rapidly changing world and its determination to navigate complex global challenges.

In the end, Qatar's story is a testament to the power of vision, leadership, and resilience in shaping a better future. It is an inspiration not only for its citizens but for nations and individuals worldwide. The odyssey of Qatar is an ongoing journey, a story that never truly ends, serving as a beacon of hope, progress, and innovation for generations to come.